COCKROACHES

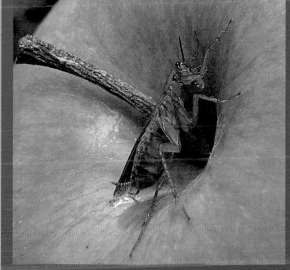

A TRUE BOOK

by

Larry Dane Brimner

Children's Press®
A Division of Grolier Publishing
New York London Hong Kong Sydney
Danbury, Connecticut

Close-up view
of a cockroach

Subject Consultant
Jeffrey Hahn
*Associate Professor
University of Minnesota
Extension Service
Department of Entomology*

Reading Consultant
Linda Cornwell
*Coordinator of School Quality
and Professional Improvement
Indiana State Teachers
Association*

Author's Dedication
*For kids everywhere
who love bugs*

**Visit Children's Press® on the
Internet at:
http://publishing.grolier.com**

Library of Congress Cataloging-in-Publication Data

Brimner, Larry Dane.
    Cockroaches / by Larry Dane Brimner.
        p.   cm. — (A true book)
    Includes bibliographical references and index.
    Summary: Describes the physical characteristics and behavior of cock-
roaches and discusses some of the different kinds.
    ISBN 0-516-21159-5 (lib. bdg.)   0-516-26758-2 (pbk.)
    1. Cockroaches—Juvenile literature.   [1. Cockroaches.]
I. Title. II. Series.
QL505.5.875 1999
595.7'28—dc21

                                                    99-13838
                                                    CIP
                                                    AC

GROLIER
PUBLISHING

Contents

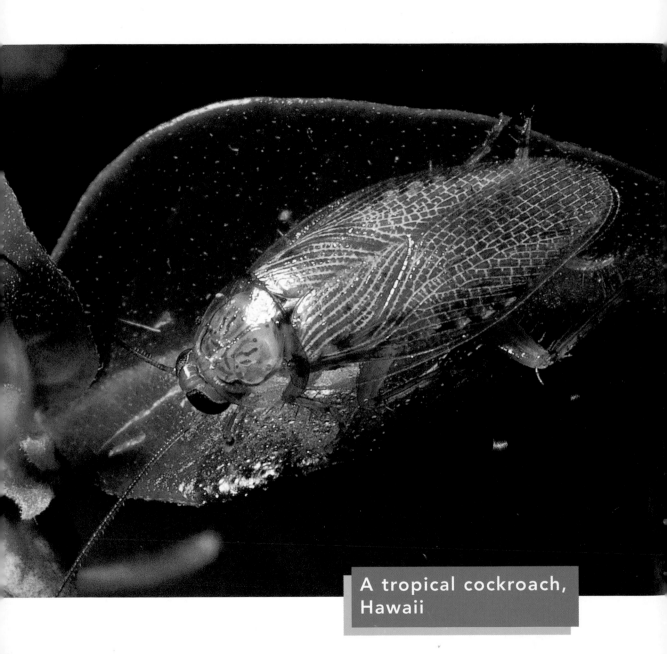

A tropical cockroach,
Hawaii

Living Fossils

Cockroaches have been around for at least 350 million years. They were living on Earth long before there were people—and even before there were dinosaurs! Cockroaches are among the oldest insects on the planet.

Scientists know this because they have found fossils of early cockroaches. Fossils are the remains of plants and animals that lived millions of years ago. They are like footprints in rock—the marks and patterns left behind by leaves or bones.

By studying the fossils of early cockroaches, scientists learned how long these insects have been living on Earth. They also learned that cockroaches have not changed much in all those millions of years. Because of this,

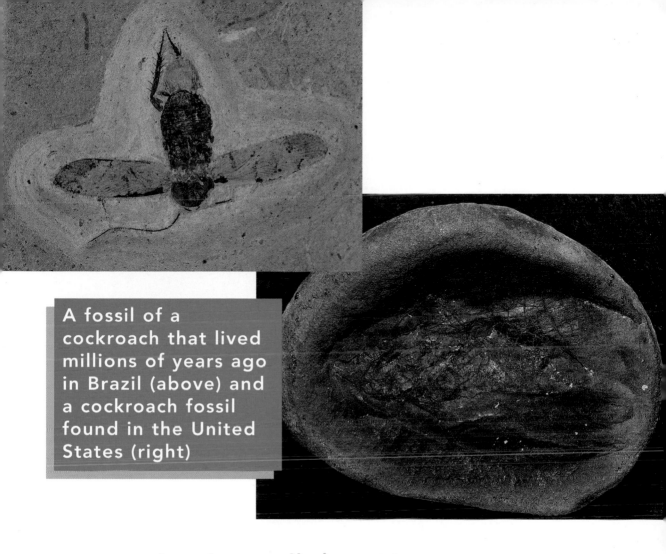

A fossil of a cockroach that lived millions of years ago in Brazil (above) and a cockroach fossil found in the United States (right)

scientists call these insects "living fossils"—animals that have survived almost unchanged since early times.

Up Close

Cockroaches are easy to recognize. They have two long feelers, or antennae, on their head. These wave around almost constantly. Cockroaches use their antennae to taste, smell, and touch what is around them.

Like all insects, a cockroach has an exoskeleton—a hard

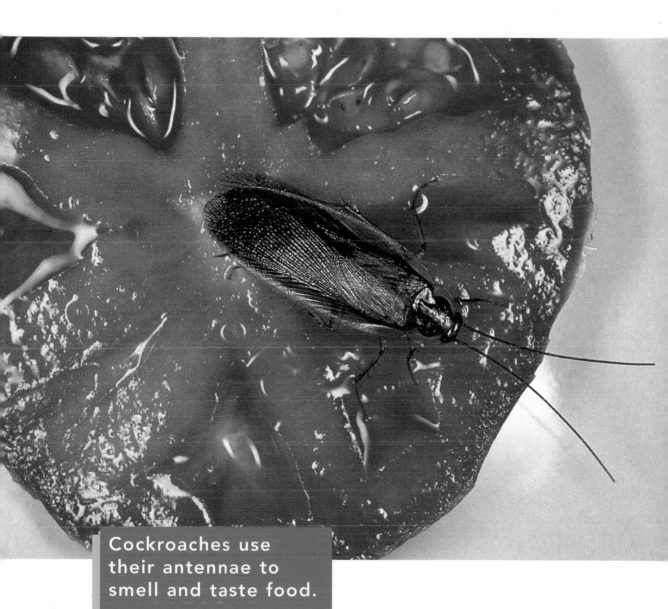

Cockroaches use their antennae to smell and taste food.

A cockroach's exoskeleton is flat and waxy-looking.

shell that helps protect its body. It's like a suit of armor. A cockroach's suit of armor is flat, waxy, and oval-shaped. It varies in color from black to different shades of brown.

A cockroach's body has three parts: the head, the thorax, and the abdomen. All insects have these three parts.

A cockroach's body has three parts: head, thorax, and abdomen.

Head **Thorax** **Abdomen**

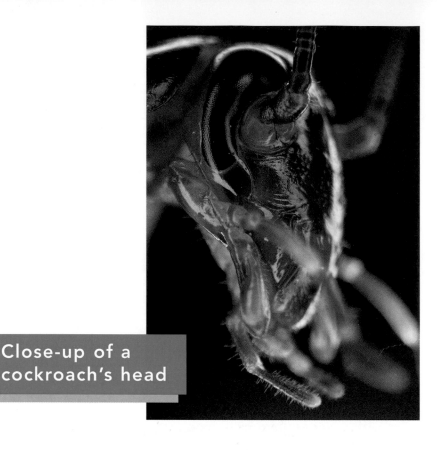

A cockroach's head is tilted
under its body. Two large
eyes cover most of its head.
These eyes are called com-
pound eyes, because each is
made up of many small parts,

called facets. Each facet is like a separate eye, so a cockroach can see in many directions at once. Some kinds of cockroaches also have two extra eyes near the base of each antenna.

Even with all its ability to see, a cockroach depends more on its antennae than on its eyes. This is because its antennae can tell it where water is located, and a cockroach needs water to survive.

A cockroach can and will eat nearly anything. It uses its strong teeth and jaws, or mandibles, to bite and crush its food. Its tongue licks up liquids. Four small feelers

A cockroach eating food left behind by humans

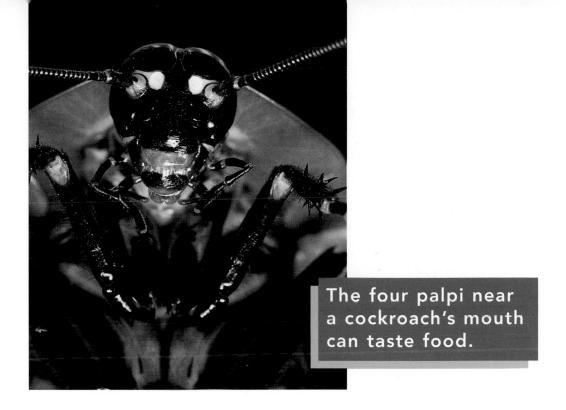

The four palpi near a cockroach's mouth can taste food.

near its mouth, called palpi, taste food even before the food reaches a cockroach's mouth.

Behind the head is the thorax. Three pairs of long, thin legs are attached to the thorax. These legs are covered with stiff hairs,

The legs of cockroaches are covered with stiff hairs (left). A close-up of the claws at the end of a cockroach's leg (right)

and each leg ends in two claws. The cockroach can hold onto almost any surface with these claws.

Many kinds of cockroaches have two pairs of wings. But even cockroaches with wings hardly ever fly. When they do, their

flights are more like short jumps. Cockroaches prefer life on the ground. When they sense danger, they usually run.

The abdomen is the largest part of a cockroach. It looks like a leathery shell and is made up of several overlapping sections.

Survivors

Cockroaches are built for survival. Their strong legs help them flee from danger. Their flat bodies help them hide in narrow places. They may not always see danger with their eyes, but they can detect it in other ways.

18

Cockroaches' flat bodies help them hide in narrow places.

The joints in a cockroach's legs are sensitive to vibrations. So its joints tell a

The cerci are two small feelers at the rear of the cockroach.

cockroach when someone or something is approaching.

At the back of the abdomen are cerci—two small pointed feelers that also sense vibrations. In addition, they sense sound and even air movements. When they do, they trigger the insect's legs to move. No wonder cockroaches are survivors—they are natural escape artists!

A Look Inside

Like all living things, cockroaches need nutrients and air to survive. When a cockroach needs nutrients, a substance called "fat body" sends some into its blood. Fat body is not blood, though. It is a white tissue that fills most of the insect's body and contains the

A scientist studying
cockroaches

Bye-Bye, Baby

After a female cockroach mates, an egg case called an ootheca forms at the rear of her body. (The Madagascar hissing cockroach is an exception—it gives birth to live young). Usually, an ootheca holds sixteen or more eggs, but the ootheca of a German cockroach may have as many as forty-eight eggs! The female carries the ootheca for a while and then drops it in a safe, dark place. After that, it's "bye-bye, baby" and the female goes on her way.

A female cockroach carrying an ootheca

She will produce several oothece during her lifetime.

   To hatch, the ootheca opens. The young cockroaches, or nymphs, scurry into the world ready to care for themselves. They are small, white, and have no wings. But there's no mistaking— they're cockroaches!

Cockroach oothece

Cockroach nymphs emerging from an ootheca

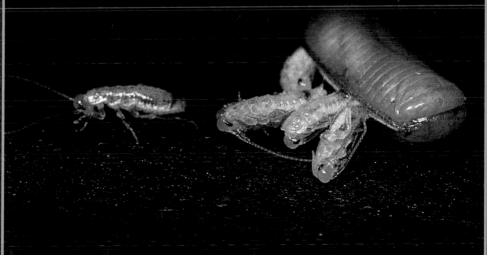

Kinds of Cockroaches

More than 3,500 different kinds, or species, of cockroaches are found throughout the world. Most of them live outside in natural surroundings, and only a very few species share shelter with people.

One of the most common cockroaches is the German

Giant South American cockroach

Madagascar hissing cockroach

African cockroach

Australian cockroach

Lapland cockroach

German cockroaches

cockroach. This is the kind of cockroach usually found in houses in North America, but it is also found in all parts of the world. German cockroaches like the warmth and moisture found in bathrooms and kitchens. They can also be found in grocery bags and old clothes.

The German cockroach is about .5 inch (1.3 cm) long. The adult is pale brown in color and has two dark stripes just behind its head. Both males and females have wings, but they prefer life on the ground. These cockroaches multiply quickly. As many as three or four generations may be produced in one year.

Oriental cockroach

The black beetle, or Oriental cockroach, is also found worldwide. It prefers cooler temperatures and often lives in damp basements, near toilets, or outdoors. It is about 1 inch (2.5 cm) long and is reddish-brown to black in color. Like the German cockroach, the Oriental cockroach lives about five or six months.

The large American cockroach probably came from Africa and is found in many

American cockroach

parts of the world. These reddish-brown insects are 1.5 to 2 inches (3.8 to 5 cm) in length and can live a year or longer. During that time, they produce many, many offspring.

Pest or Helper?

Cockroaches lead very dull lives by human standards. They live in dark cracks and out-of-the-way places. They rest for at least eighteen hours a day. Then they scurry around looking for food. But are they the pests many people believe they are?

Cockroaches rest during the day and look for food at night.

Cockroaches are not known to carry diseases. True, if they live in a dirty place, they can *spread* the germs that cause diseases.

This is because they are not picky eaters. For example, they might eat out of your cat's litter box one minute and walk across your kitchen counter the next.

Cockroaches swarming over an unwashed dinner plate

A cockroach in search of food

Cockroaches leave behind their waste, or feces, wherever they go. They also have a nasty habit of vomiting part of the food they eat. It's no wonder that cockroaches leave behind a bad smell. People who suffer from asthma or allergies are often allergic to household cockroaches.

Yet these unexciting survivors play a role in the careful balance of nature. Most cockroaches live outdoors, where

Although people think of cockroaches as indoor pests, most cockroaches actually live outdoors.

they help rid the world of waste. They are nature's recyclers. Chances are they will continue to recycle for as long as Earth survives.

Ready, Set, Go!

Imagine a tractor pull with cockroaches. It happens! At Purdue University in Indiana, Madagascar hissing cockroaches com-peted in a tractor pull. These cockroaches are giants that can grow up to 2 to 3 inches (5 to 7.5 cm) long.

Madagascar hissing cockroach

A cockroach race on an American college campus

Of course, the trac-tors were miniature toys.

In Australia, cockroach races are a yearly event. The track is a tube in the shape of—you guessed it—Australia!

To Find Out More

Here are some additional resources to help you learn more about cockroaches:

 **Books**

Becker, Christine, and Kidd, Nina. **Cockroaches, Stinkbugs, and Other Creepy Crawlers** (Draw Science series). Contemporary Books, 1996.

Facklam, Margery. **The Big Bug Book.** Little Brown & Co., 1994.

Green, Tamara. **Cockroaches** (The New Creepy Crawly Collection). Gareth Stevens Publishing, 1997.

Kerby, Mona. **Cockroaches.** Franklin Watts, 1989.

Llewellyn, Claire. **The Best Book of Bugs.** Larousse Kingfisher Chambers, 1998.

Mound, Lawrence. **Amazing Insects.** Knopf, 1993.

Wiseman, Stella. **Cockroach** (Pocket Pests series). Little Simon, 1997.

☼ Organizations and Online Sites

Bug Club
http://www.ex.ac.uk/ bugclub/

This is the webpage of the Amateur Entomologists' Society's Bug Club for Young Entomologists, a British club devoted to young people who are fascinated by bugs. It provides a newsletter, lists club events, and includes a page on how to keep cockroaches as pets.

Get this Bug off of Me!
http://www.uky.edu/ Agriculture/Entomology/ ythfacts/hurtrnot.htm

This site, sponsored by the University of Kentucky, describes common insects—including cockroaches—that, though scary-looking, don't hurt humans.

Young Entomologists' Society, Inc.
6907 West Grand River Avenue
Lansing, MI 48906

An organization that provides publications and outreach programs for young people interested in insect study.

Yucky Bug World
http://www. yucky.com/ roaches/

This site, devoted to cockroaches, includes information on cockroach anatomy, a fun "day in the life of a cockroach," amazing roach facts, photos of various kinds of cockroaches, and a glossary of important terms relating to cockroaches.

45

Important Words

cerci small, sensitive hairs at the back end of a cockroach that warn of anything sneaking up behind the cockroach

detect find; notice

generation group of living things born around the same time

joint point in an animal's body where two or more parts or bones are joined

mandibles mouthparts that hold or bite food

multiply to become more in number

nutrients substances, like vitamins and minerals, that provide health and good growth

palpi small feelers near a cockroach's mouth that can taste food

vibration rapid or quivering motion from side to side

Index

Meet the Author

Larry Dane Brimner is a former teacher who now writes full time for children. He has written many books for Children's Press, including *The World Wide Web*, *E-mail*, *Polar Mammals*, and *The Winter Olympics*. He lives in the American southwest.

RAP

10-20-00

GAYLORD FG